Yao Ming

Basketball's Big Man

Titles in the **SPORTS LEADERS** *Series:*

Vince Carter
0-7660-2173-4

Allen Iverson
0-7660-2174-2

Derek Jeter
0-7660-2035-5

Jason Kidd
0-7660-2214-5

Lisa Leslie
0-7660-2423-7

Shaquille O'Neal
0-7660-2175-0

Yao Ming

Basketball's Big Man

Jeff C. Young

Enslow Publishers, Inc.
40 Industrial Road   PO Box 38
Box 398   Aldershot
Berkeley Heights, NJ 07922   Hants GU12 6BP
USA   UK
http://www.enslow.com

To my friend, Dale Reecy. Thanks for taking me to see Yao play.

Library of Congress Cataloging-in-Publication Data

Young, Jeff C., 1948-
    Yao Ming : basketball's big man / Jeff C. Young.— 1st ed.
      p. cm. — (Sports leaders series)
    Includes bibliographical references and index.
    ISBN 0-7660-2422-9
    1. Yao, Ming, 1980– —Juvenile literature. 2. Basketball players—China—
Biography—Juvenile literature. I. Title. II. Series.
    GV884.Y36Y68 2004
    796.323'092—dc22

                              2004012151

Printed in the United States of America

10 9 8 7 6 5 4 3 2 1

To Our Readers:
We have done our best to make sure all Internet addresses in this book were active and
appropriate when we went to press. However, the author and the publisher have no control over and assume no liability for the material available on those Internet sites or on
other Web sites they may link to. Any comments or suggestions can be sent by e-mail to
comments@enslow.com or to the address on the back cover.

Illustration Credits: Alex Livesey/Allsport, p. 32; Andrew D. Bernstein/
NBAE via Getty Images, pp. 72, 90; Bill Baptist/NBAE/Getty Images, pp. 6,
10, 18, 52, 55, 74; CREDIT Stephen Dunn/Getty Images, p. 88; D. Clarke
Evans/NBAE via Getty Images, p. 84; David Sherman/NBAE/Getty Images,
pp. 48, 66; Garrett Ellwood/NBAE via Getty Images, p. 82; Glen James/
NBAE/Getty Images, pp. 61, 64; Jamie Squire/NBAE/Getty Images, p. 13; Jed
Jacobsohn/Allsport, p. 22; Jeff Reinking/NBAE/Getty Images, p. 69; Jonathan
Daniel/Getty Images, p. 37; Layne Murdoch/NBAE/Getty Images, p. 59; Lisa
Blumenfeld/Getty Images, p. 80; Nathaniel S. Butler/NBAE via Getty Images,
p. 24; Otto Greule, Jr./Getty Images, p. 45; Stephen Dunn/Getty Images,
p. 77; Tim DeFrisco/Allsport, p. 41; Vincent Laforet/ NBAE via Getty Images,
p. 29.

Cover Illustration: David Sherman/NBAE/Getty Images.

CONTENTS

A GIANT MATCHUP

It did not seem like a fair matchup, having the Houston Rockets rookie center Yao Ming posting up against the NBA's premier player in the paint and perennial all-star, Shaquille O'Neal.

Shaq was a veteran of over 750 regular season and playoff games. Yao would be playing in only his thirty-eighth regular season NBA game. Yao was four inches taller and eight years younger, but Shaq outweighed Yao by over thirty pounds. Shaq often used that weight advantage to bump and knock opposing players out of his way. Shaq had helped lead the Los Angeles Lakers to three NBA titles in a row. During those three years Shaq was the Most Valuable Player

(MVP) of the championship series each year. The Rockets had not even made the playoffs during that three-year span.

In September of 2002, ESPN's David Aldridge asked Yao what he would expect during his first game against Shaq. Yao thoughtfully replied, "I think it will be one-sided in my matchup against Shaquille O'Neal. He is much better than I at this point. I think that the NBA is a very good classroom for me. I think that I will learn from defeat and from my setbacks, and it will set a foundation for me to improve in the future."[1]

Overshadowing the marquee matchup between the league's superstar center and the highly publicized rookie were racially insensitive remarks Shaq had made months earlier.In June of 2002, the Rockets had made Yao the first non-American player ever chosen first in the NBA draft. In a radio interview shortly after draft day, Shaq mocked Yao by saying, "Tell Yao Ming, ching, chong, yang wah ah so."[2]

Shaq intended for his remarks to be taken as a joke, but many Asians did not think it was funny. Two weeks before the game, the publication *Asian Week* scolded Shaq for his insensitivity. Shaq apologized in Chinese by using the Mandarin word, *dui bu qi*, which means "I'm sorry."[3]

Yao was more concerned about the upcoming game than about some silly remark Shaq had made months before. He viewed the incident as a cultural difference. "I think that there are a lot of difficulties in two different cultures understanding each other," Yao said, "especially countries of very large populations [such as] China and the United States. The world is getting smaller and has a greater understanding of cultures. I believe Shaquille O'Neal was joking with what he said, but a lot of Asian people don't understand this kind of joke."[4]

> "I will learn from defeat . . . and [will] improve in the future."
> —Yao Ming

On January 17, 2003, the time for talking and joking was over. A crowd of 16,285 fans filled Houston's Compaq Center to watch the heralded rookie face off against the dominating veteran. Millions of others watched the game on television. It was broadcast nationally in both the United States and China. The game became the highest-rated basketball program ever broadcast on ESPN.

The Lakers wasted no time in testing Yao. On their first possession they passed the ball to Shaq. He was to the right of the basket, about twenty feet away, when he began driving to the baseline. After dribbling by Yao, Shaq went up for a shot. Yao

Yao Ming shoots over Shaquille O'Neal during a game at the Compaq Center in Houston, Texas, on January 17, 2003.

quickly moved beside him and blocked Shaq's shot attempt.

After stopping Shaq defensively, Yao challenged him offensively. He followed the blocked shot by sinking a sweeping sky hook at the other end of the floor.

About two minutes into the game, Shaq positioned himself for a dunk. He dribbled twice, and then made a spin move for the hoop. Once again, Yao was there to stop him. In less than two minutes he had blocked two of Shaq's shots.

Yao followed the block by hustling on offense. In transition he beat Shaq down the floor. Rockets point guard Steve Francis saw Yao open and cutting for the basket. A pinpoint pass by Francis allowed Yao to bank the ball off the glass. Houston took a 6–2 lead.

On the Lakers' next possession Shaq was in the low post position, four feet from the basket. Yao posted up and Shaq made contact, hoping to push Yao out of position. Yao was able to maintain his defensive stance, and he jumped when Shaq spinned toward the hoop. Another block! In three minutes Yao had blocked three of Shaq's shots.

Playing against someone with Shaq's size and strength will eventually wear you down. Yao was no exception. Later in the game Shaq would back into Yao and make two rim-rattling dunks. When he did, Yao would run upcourt and focus on making the transition to offense.

By the game's end Shaq had both outscored (31–10) and outrebounded Yao (13–10). But the Rockets won in overtime, 108–104. No player is going to dominate Shaq, but Yao held his own against him long enough for the Rockets to win.

Sports Illustrated's NBA writer Marty Burns offered this evaluation: "For Yao, the most important thing Friday was to survive. He didn't have to win the matchup; he just had to avoid getting embarrassed. From that standpoint, he was a huge success."[5]

Rockets coach Rudy Tomjanovich saw Yao's showdown with Shaq as something to build on for a bright future: "I thought he did a great job," the coach said. "No one can stop Shaq, you just can't. But we got to play our game, too. I thought [Yao] had a very good beginning of the game. Then he got a little tentative offensively, just tried to get his shot over with too quick. But it was a great learning experience."[6]

In his first twenty-six games of the 2003 NBA season, Shaq had only had twelve of his shots blocked. In his first confrontation with Yao, Shaq had five shots blocked. Shaq graciously acknowledged

Yao Ming blocks the shot of the Lakers' Shaquille O'Neal during the highly anticipated game that took place on January 17, 2003. Yao blocked three of O'Neal's shots in the first three minutes of the game.

Yao's skills but also made it clear that he would not be intimidated.

"He's 7-5," Shaq said. "He's supposed to block my shots. He's a good player. He's 7-5 and he plays big. I have nothing derogatory to say about him. That's not the first time in my career that my shot has been blocked by a shot-blocker. The key is to just keep coming at him."[7]

After the game Yao admitted that Shaq's strategy of constant attack took its toll. "I've never encountered someone that strong before," Yao said. "He's not crafty. It's just strength. It wore me out playing him."[8]

While showing the world that he clearly belonged in the NBA and that he could compete with the best, Yao put things in perspective. It was only one win with forty-four regular season games left. "How should I put it?" Yao asked. "We beat the Lakers today. Shaq is still Shaq."[9]

GROWING UP

As a boy growing up in Shanghai, China, Yao Ming's life was not dominated by hoop dreams. Yao was a passive and shy child who avoided being picked on by retreating into books. Instead of fighting battles with his fists, he read about them, poring over books about military history. He dreamed about travel and adventure rather than basketball stardom. "I wanted to be an adventurer and explore the world," Yao said.[1]

Yao played a little basketball after his parents taught him the game. His father, Yao Zhi Yuan, was a 6–7 forward on the Chinese Men's National Team. His mother, Fang Feng Di, was a 6–3 captain and center of the Chinese Women's National Team. Yao learned the game just for fun, not because he planned on making it his career. "My parents didn't teach me basketball like it was a profession," Yao said. "They taught me for fun."[2]

Yao's parents wisely decided to let him decide if basketball was going to be an important part of his life. They never pressured him to play or practice. "My parents have a lot to do with why I am good at basketball," Yao admitted. "But they never told me that I had to play. They told me to do what I wanted to do."[3]

Because of his exceptional height, Yao was expected to become an exceptional athlete. When Yao was nine years old, he was already over 5 ½ feet tall. One day his teacher asked his class which student in their class could make a free throw. His classmates eagerly responded, "Yao!" At that time, Yao knew he was not as good as they thought. "I couldn't shoot at all," Yao recalled. "I could only make a layup if no one else was around."[4]

By the time he was twelve, Yao was 6–6 and attracting the attention of Chinese government officials who trained athletes for Olympic and international competition. He was enrolled at the provincial sports academy. But he was not recruited to play basketball. He was placed on their water polo team. "I played water polo for two months," Yao said, "but they kicked me off the team because my skill level was too far behind. I couldn't swim fast enough."[5]

Yao turned to other sports, but basketball became his favorite. When he was fourteen, he qualified for a tryout to make Shanghai's junior team. He left home and entered a new environment, one in which hoops would become his world. It was like a basketball boot camp.

"We had to be on the court at six in the morning," Yao recalled. "We wouldn't eat breakfast first. We'd go distance running. After running, you would have to make one hundred shots. Then you would eat breakfast and rest for a little while. Half an hour later you would resume practicing."[6]

Three times a week, they would practice for up to ten hours a day. He had no life outside of basketball. On Sundays he was allowed a day off to visit his parents, but all he felt like doing was eating and resting. On Monday, Yao would return for another six hard days of intensive practice and exercise.

"That kind of training doesn't exist anymore," Yao said. "I was unlucky I was in the last group to have to do that. At that time, I guess I really didn't

Yao Ming (far right) is escorted through Houston Intercontinental Airport by (left to right) Rockets General Manager Carroll Dawson, his mother, Fang Feng Di, and his father, Yao Zi Yuan. Both of Yao's parents were Olympic basketball players.

have a choice. If I had to do it again, I don't think I could do it."[7]

But even with his basketball genes and awesome height, Yao was not a great natural player. His first coach, Li Zhangming, remembered Yao as being awkward and not overly enthusiastic about the game. "He didn't like basketball very much in the beginning. He was so much taller than the other kids and an awkward mover. It took time to cultivate his interest, by playing games and making him feel the fun of basketball."[8]

While Yao was receiving his first formal basketball

coaching and training at the Youth Sports School, the NBA began broadcasting its games on Chinese television. In June of 1994, Yao saw his first NBA game when the New York Knicks and Houston Rockets played for the NBA Championship. Yao became an avid NBA fan. Like kids and NBA fans all over the world, Yao would try to imitate the moves of pro basketball stars he watched on TV. "I liked watching Charles Barkley, Hakeen Olajuwon . . . and of course I knew Michael Jordan."[9]

When he was fourteen, Yao was selected to play on the Shanghai Oriental Sharks in the junior league of the Chinese Basketball Association (CBA). One year later, the Houston Rockets began scouting Yao.

By his sixteenth birthday Yao was over 7 feet tall. As Yao grew, so did interest in him as an emerging basketball star. He attracted the attention of Terry Rhoads, who was Nike's director of marketing in China. Rhoads was so impressed with Yao that he invited him to a Nike basketball camp in Paris, France, in the summer of 1997. "Our guys in the U.S. didn't believe that there was a Chinese kid that tall," Rhoads recalled. "Once we convinced them, they invited us to bring him to a Nike camp in Paris that summer. This was the first time he was matching up against players his own age, and he stood out."[10]

Del Harris, then the head coach of the Milwaukee Bucks, was attending the camp. He was very impressed by Yao's skills. Harris predicted: "one day he's going to have a real impact in the NBA."[11]

By his seventeenth birthday, Yao was 7-foot-3 and began attracting worldwide attention. At the Asian Basketball Championship for Junior Men he was named the most valuable player. Then, American basketball fans got to see Yao when he attended Nike's All-American Basketball Camp in Indianapolis, Indiana. Yao also played for the Nike-sponsored Association of American Universities (AAU) team High Five America.

> "One day he's going to have a real impact in the NBA."
> —Del Harris

The 2000 Olympics in Sydney, Australia, gave Yao his first experience playing against seasoned NBA veterans. NBA stars Jason Kidd, Kevin Garnett, Vince Carter, Tim Hardaway, and Gary Payton led the American team to the gold medal. They were coached by Rudy Tomjanovich, who would later become Yao's first NBA coach.

Although China lost to the United States, 119–72, Yao performed impressively. Early in the game Yao and 7-1 Wang Zhizhi, who was China's first NBA player, briefly disrupted the American team. China took an early 13–7 lead before the USA squad took control.

"I thought the first few minutes of the game, we did not adjust to their size," Tomjanovich said. "Their 7-footers affected the game defensively by stepping into our lane."[12]

The Chinese team posted a 2–4 record in the Olympics, but Yao's play attracted a worldwide audience. He averaged 10.5 points, 6.0 rebounds, and 2.2 blocked shots per game. Yao also led his team in shooting percentage (.639). NBA scouts were impressed by Yao's agility and soft shooting touch.

Basketball commentator and NBA Hall of Fame player Bill Walton was awed by Yao's Olympic performance. Writing in *ESPN The Magazine*, Walton said:

> After watching Yao Ming compete against the best players in the world, I left Sydney dizzy with the possibilities. Simply put, the twenty-year-old Yao has a chance to alter the way the game of basketball is played. . . . This guy has skills, competitiveness, and basketball intelligence that far exceed his limited background. As I watched his crisp and imaginative passes, felt the energy surge when he'd whip an outlet to launch a fast break, and noted his decision making and great court demeanor, I knew I was peering into the future. . . . Yes, Yao is a

Yao Ming attempts to block the shot of Alonzo Mourning during the 2000 Olympic Games in Sydney, Australia.

work-in-progress, but if I were an NBA coach, I'd make him my work-in-progress.[13]

The following summer, Yao was able to lead the Chinese team to a prestigious championship. At the Asian Basketball Championship for Men, Yao averaged 13.4 points, 10.1 rebounds, and 2.8 blocks while playing only about twenty minutes a game. He was voted the tournament's MVP.

In August of 2001, Yao helped China win a silver (second place) medal in the World University Games at Beijing, China. In the semifinal round China scored a historic victory by ending the USA's forty-six-game winning streak in World University Games competition.

In the 2002 Asian Games at Busan, South Korea, Yao and his teammates suffered a surprising and disappointing defeat. In the championship game they lost to South Korea, 102–100. It was a humbling loss for China. The last time they had lost a championship game was in 1982, when Yao was two years old. Yao could hardly be blamed for China's unexpected loss. He scored 23 points and had 22 rebounds.

A year after the loss in the Asian Games, Yao led China to a payback win against South Korea. Playing before mostly home team fans in Beijing, China beat South Korea, 106–96. The victory secured a spot for

Wang Zhizhi of the Miami Heat drives to the hoop during a game against the New York Knicks in January 2004. Wang was the first Chinese player to play in the NBA.

China in men's basketball at the 2004 Olympics in Athens. Yao sparked the win with a 30-point, 15-rebound performance.

As the 2001–02 NBA season approached, Yao's Olympic teammates Wang Zhizhi and Mengke Bateer were playing in the NBA. Yao would be joining them if NBA officials could persuade the Chinese government to allow it.

3

SWIMMING WITH THE SHARKS

In the 1997–98 season Yao made his pro debut with the Shanghai Sharks in the Chinese Basketball Association. As a seventeen-year-old rookie, Yao averaged 10.0 points and 8.3 rebounds a game in twenty-one games. It was an impressive debut considering his lack of experience.

Yao's second season in the CBA was cut short because of a leg fracture. He only played in twelve games, but he more than doubled his scoring average (20.9) and improved his rebounding average to 12.9 per game. Yao also began to emerge as a defensive star. His average of 2.5 blocked shots per game was second in the CBA.

The 1999–2000 season was Yao's third year in the CBA. Now, at the age of nineteen, he was considered one of the best players in the league. He led the CBA in rebounding (14.6), blocked shots (2.5 per game), and dunks (55). Yao was sixth in the league in scoring (21.2 ppg) and seventh in steals with a 2.4 per game average.

Although the Sharks failed to win the CBA championship, Yao had become one of the league's most dominating players. Still, there were detractors who pointed out the level of play in the CBA was not equal to that of the NBA. Until he faced NBA competition, Yao would be regarded as an outstanding player in an inferior league.

Yao's hopes of showcasing his talents outside of the CBA were dashed when the Chinese government barred him from playing in the Nike Hoop Summit in Indianapolis, Indiana. The event was scheduled for the last weekend in March of 2000. Indianapolis was also hosting the NCAA's Men's Basketball Final Four playoffs that weekend. There would be many NBA coaches and agents looking to recruit and sign new international players.

Since Yao had been chosen to play on China's Olympic basketball team, the Chinese government would not let him leave the country. Xu Minfeng, director of the CBA's general office, issued a statement declaring:"Yao Ming has been chosen for China's national Olympic team and must start intensive training in Beijing on April 1."[1]

Minfeng said there was also another reason. He said Yao could not leave China because he "has played a lot of games in the past year, feels very tired, and needs time to recover."[2]

During the 1999–2000 CBA season Yao played in thirty-three games. That's about the same number of games that a college team winning the NCAA Championship would play. An NBA team advancing to the league's championship round plays one hundred or more games in a season. If Yao needed rest and a break from basketball, he was not going to get it by practicing for the Olympics.

Yao made no public comments about the government's decision, but it was believed that he was deeply disappointed. A Chinese paper, the *Jinan Times*, quoted Yao as saying, "What a big shame! This is my last chance."[3]

In 2001 Yao would not be eligible for the next Nike Basketball Summit. Yao was able to put his disappointment behind him and focused on the Olympics. He played well, but the Chinese team lost

Yao Ming dribbles the ball during a game at the Nike Basketball Camp on July 9, 1998, in Indianapolis, Indiana. The Chinese government would not allow Yao to attend a similar event in March of 2000.

four of six games and finished in tenth place. After a short rest, it was time for another season in the CBA.

Although he was only twenty years old, Yao had become one of the most dominant players in the CBA. That dominance continued throughout the 2000–01 season. He averaged 27.1 points and 19.4 rebounds per game, along with 5.5 blocked shots. Yao led the Sharks into the CBA finals against the Bayi Rockets.

In postseason play Yao was even more dominating. He led the Sharks to a three-games-to-one CBA championship series against the Rockets. In the Sharks 123–122 championship win, Yao came within 3 blocked shots of having a triple-double (double figures in three different categories) with 44 points, 21 rebounds, and 7 blocked shots. Yao's most impressive accomplishment in the championship game was probably his shooting. He was perfect, making 21 shots in 21 attempts.

But there were other events going on that would have a greater impact on Yao's basketball future than a CBA title. The Chinese government was finally agreeing to let its best basketball players play in the NBA. In 1999 Wang Zhizhi was a second-round draft pick of the Dallas Mavericks. In 2002 Mengke Bateer was signed by the Denver Nuggets. There was little doubt that Yao would be joining them and become the third Chinese player in the NBA.

However, Yao would be turning pro under a surprising new set of regulations by the Chinese government. The new government regulations would cost Yao millions of dollars. Two months before the 2002 NBA draft, the Chinese government decreed that Chinese athletes playing outside of China would have to turn over at least half of their pretax income to Chinese government agencies. That included money made from endorsements and commercials.

Some superstar athletes like Shaquille O'Neal and Tiger Woods make more money from endorsements than they do from playing their sport. Yao and his family were reportedly stunned by the new regulations. Once again, Yao was disappointed, but he took the news graciously.

"I have endured so much frustration, a little more won't beat me," Yao said.[4]

Yao had no choice but to go along. If he refused, Yao would have faced fines, expulsion from China's national team, and attempts by the government to void his contract with any NBA team that drafted him.

There were still other obstacles to Yao's playing in the NBA. His agent had to be Chinese and had to

Yao Ming meets tennis star Andre Agassi at an event to promote kids day at the Heineken Open in Shanghai, China, on September 17, 2001.

be registered as an agent with the CBA. The new rules also said that Yao could not leave China until his NBA contract was approved by his Chinese agent, the Shanghai Sharks, the local government sports bureau, and the CBA.

Thirty percent of Yao's pretax earnings would go to the CBA. Another 10 percent would go to the Chinese central government's State Sports Administration. Still another 10 percent was earmarked for the Shanghai government. The remaining 50 percent would be split between Yao, the Shanghai Sharks, his Chinese coaches, and his agent.

Still, Yao was eagerly awaiting draft day. After enduring setbacks and frustrations, he would finally be getting a chance to play and compete with the best professional basketball players in the world. Over half of his salary was a comparatively small price to pay for the privilege of playing in the NBA.

NUMBER
ONE PICK

In May of 2002, the Houston Rockets, who had the first pick in the upcoming NBA draft, began serious talks with the Chinese government about drafting Yao. Coach Rudy Tomjanovich, along with the team's general manager and legal counsel, flew to China to negotiate for Yao's services. After three days of detailed bargaining, the Rockets hoped that they finally had a deal.

Still, they did not know for sure until the morning of draft day. On June 26, Rockets legal counsel, Michael Goldberg, received a letter verifying that Yao was eligible for the NBA draft. He quickly called Houston's general manager, Carroll Dawson.

"I thought I'd scream, but I just fell back in bed and stared at the ceiling," Dawson said. "I felt such a great relief. The whole franchise wanted this so badly. I just felt that it would all be worked out."[1]

Yao's deep desire to play in the NBA was well known. After showcasing his talents at a predraft workout in Chicago, Yao issued a statement: "It's been a dream of mine to play in the NBA ever since I saw a game on TV many years ago. To almost touch that dream today fills me with a sense of joy that words simply cannot describe. I am humbled and grateful for the unforgettable experience the past few days."[2]

Yao went on to thank Chicago and then the NBA, along with all the teams that showed an interest in him. Then, Yao thanked the fans by adding, "Last, but certainly not least, I owe the greatest debt of gratitude to fans of basketball everywhere. You gave me the greatest job on earth. And I promise to repay your trust by respecting the game and by challenging myself to be the best that I can be."[3] Yao ended his statement on an upbeat note: "Let the good times roll!"[4]

On June 26, draft day, the Houston Rockets made Yao the first player chosen in the 2002 NBA draft. They were delighted to be gaining his services, but several sportswriters were very critical of their decision. Some of the criticisms were very harsh.

ESPN's outspoken basketball commentator Dick Vitale said, "My gut feeling tells me the Rockets are making a mistake, baby, in evaluating their overall No. 1 pick. Still, Rudy T. could shock America by having NBA commissioner David Stern announce [Jay] Williams's name as the top pick. Then Houston would be moving in the right direction."[5]

Vitale's ESPN colleague Bill Simmons was even harsher. He said that Yao being chosen before Williams would be remembered as an NBA draft day blunder. Simmons was so sure that Yao would fail, he said, "I'm just not predicting it, I'm guaranteeing it."[6]

Memphis sportswriter Ron Millery was another critic of the Rockets' first round pick. He ridiculed Yao by writing, "They call Yao Ming 'The Next Big Thing,' but he looks like the 'Next Big Stiff.' . . . The Chinese government may want to go to war after Shaquille O'Neal puts a hole in Yao's chest. He'll have an average NBA career."[7]

If those critics had read some of the reports on Yao from the pro scouts, they might not have been so quick to put him down. In Yao's profile on nbadraft.net, Yao was rated in twelve categories: athleticism, defense, quickness, jump shot, rebounding,

Television analyst Dick Vitale (above) expressed strong doubts about Yao Ming's ability to succeed in the NBA.

post skills, size, strength, leadership, readiness to play in the NBA, potential, and intangibles.

In four categories—size, jump shot, potential, and intangibles—Yao scored a perfect 10. In rebounding, post skills, readiness to play in the NBA, and leadership, Yao got 9s. His lowest score was in quickness, where he was rated a 7. Out of a possible 120 points, Yao scored 108.

The Web site listed his major strengths as his agility, athleticism, shooting, and ability to adapt to plays as they are happening. Yao's biggest weakness was the question of his eligibility to play in the NBA and concerns about possible injuries. Players of Yao's size are often prone to foot and knee problems because of stress on their joints. They predicted that Yao "may take some time to adjust to the NBA, but his upside is so tremendous he will be the top overall draft choice."[8]

Don Casey, who had coached the New Jersey Nets, had traveled to China in November of 2001 to scout Yao. He gave a glowing evaluation of Yao's skills. Casey said Yao's main strengths were his size, shooting touch, passing skills, post moves, and defensive skills. Casey also added that Yao was a great competitor and quite coachable.

Casey said Yao's major weaknesses were questions

about his strength and stamina. In the CBA the emphasis was on aerobic training instead of weight training. Casey felt Yao had to bulk up and build up more upper body strength. Casey was also uncertain if Yao could withstand the rigors of an eighty-two-game NBA season.

Still, Casey predicted: "He will hold his own in this league. . . . The biggest unknown is whether he can take the day-to-day pound-ing over the course of the season. . . . But Yao is so com-mitted to playing in the NBA, once he is in a weight program he will be able to withstand the NBA style over the long haul . . . he is an extremely hard worker and has such a tremendous upside, a player like him doesn't come around too often."[9]

> "[Yao's] upside is so tremendous he will be the top overall draft choice."
> — from nbadraft.net

Vitale and Simmons might have changed their minds if they had read what their employer said about Yao. ESPN's NBA draft tracker Web site described Yao as "very agile" and said that "even at 7-foot-6, he can get out and run the floor like a small forward. . . . He has a reliable jump hook, and has shown the ability to pass like a guard within the offense to cutting teammates. His basketball IQ isn't a question, neither is his talent. He also shot nearly 80 percent from the free throw line, which is a bonus for any big man."[10]

The only negative qualities about Yao in ESPN's scouting report were the usual concerns about his weight and strength. Some of the stronger centers in the NBA would have no trouble moving Yao out of the post. They also expressed concerns about the language barrier between Yao and his teammates, along with the time it would take for Yao to adjust to American basketball.

Former Indiana Pacers coach and New York Knicks president Isaiah Thomas predicted that Yao would have great success in the NBA.

He's not just 7-5, but a talented, active athlete and the guy is mentally tough. He has great ambition to succeed in the NBA, and he is going to. It will take a year, but he will make an impression early on. His biggest strength is shot-blocking, but he is a great passer, too. . . . He speaks decent English, so there will be no problem coaching him. Eventually he will become the best big man ever to play in the NBA.[11]

Prior to Yao there had been several exceptionally tall NBA players who had less than spectacular careers. Yao's critics were comparing him to those players even though they had not seen Yao play.

Manute Bol of the Golden State Warriors tries to prevent T. R. Dunn of the Denver Nuggets from passing the ball.

Before Yao was drafted, there had been eight players 7-4 or taller to play in the NBA. Only three of the eight were taller than Yao. Two of them, Manute Bol and Gheorghe Muresan, were 7-foot-7. Despite their great height, neither became a dominant player.

Bol twice led the NBA in blocked shots, and he still shares the NBA records for most blocked shots in a half (11) and in a quarter (8). Although he showed superior defensive skills, Bol lacked an offensive game. In 619 games he only scored 1,584 points for an average of 2.6 points per game. Bol wasn't much of a rebounder or playmaker, either. He averaged only 4.3 rebounds and less than one assist per game during his ten seasons in the NBA.

Muresan played in the NBA from 1993 to 2000. He developed a good post game with a surprisingly soft shooting touch. In the 1995–96 season he was voted the NBA's Most Improved Player for averaging 14.5 points and 9.6 rebounds per game. However, his lack of quickness and mobility limited his playing time. Recurring injuries ended Muresan's NBA career when he was only twenty-nine.

Among the players in the exclusive 7-4 and taller club, Mark Eaton had the best defensive skills and shot-blocking stats. Eaton played eleven seasons for the Utah Jazz, from 1982 to 1993. Eaton was twice named the NBA's Defensive Player of the Year, and he led the NBA in blocked shots four times. He still holds the NBA single season records for most blocked shots (456) and blocks per game (5.6).

Because he concentrated on defense, Eaton was never much of a scorer. He averaged only 6 points per game. In spite of his extreme height, Eaton averaged just under 8 rebounds per game.

Among active NBA players, Yao was most often compared to 7-foot-6 Shawn Bradley of the Dallas Mavericks. Since making his NBA debut in 1993, Bradley has become an exceptional shot-blocker. Two times he's lead the NBA in that category. Bradley has also put up respectable numbers in scoring (9.2 per game) and rebounding (7.1 per game), while only playing about twenty-six minutes a game. But Bradley has never become a dominating center like a Shaquille O'Neal or a Wilt Chamberlain.

Another criticism of Bradley is that he is too light and gets pushed out of position by the league's bulkier and more muscular centers. Even though Bradley weighs 275, that's light for someone who is 7-foot-6. When Yao was drafted, his weight was listed at 297.

Like Bol and Bradley, 7-5 Chuck Nevitt was another tall but slender player whose height made him the victim of big expectations. Nevitt played on four NBA teams in nine seasons, while playing only about five minutes a game. Nevitt noted the pressures to perform when you're that tall by saying, "You're [still] supposed to get every rebound and block every shot. If your teammates get beat out front and their man scores, they get all over you because you're supposed to come over and help. If anyone ever scored inside the paint, it was always your fault."[12]

Like Yao, 7-4 Ralph Sampson was picked by the Rockets first in the NBA draft. Sampson was picked in the 1983 NBA draft after an outstanding college career at the University of Virginia, where he was a three-time All-American. Sampson's NBA career started off promisingly. He was the NBA's Rookie of the Year in 1984. During his first three seasons Sampson averaged over 20 points and 10 rebounds a game. In 1985 he was the MVP of the NBA All-Star Game. But after three years, recurring knee problems limited Sampson's efficiency and playing time. During his final three seasons Sampson played in only sixty-one games. He retired in 1992 when he was only thirty-one.

The 7-foot 4-inch Rik Smits was born outside the United States, just as Yao was. Smits was born in Holland and during his twelve seasons in the NBA

Ralph Sampson was drafted out of college by the Houston Rockets, who expected great things from him due to his size. Here, he puts the ball up against his old team while playing for the Golden State Warriors in a game from 1989.

(1988–2000) he was known as The Dunkin' Dutchman. Although he was not a dominating player, Smits had a very good low post offensive game. He averaged 14.8 points a game while shooting over 50 percent (.507) and playing only about twenty-seven minutes a game. His weak points were a lack of mobility and poor rebounding for a player of his size (6.1 per game).

If Yao thought anything about the comparisons, he kept it to himself. He knew that everything he did on the court would be carefully scrutinized, videotaped, reported, and seen by millions of fans worldwide. When he was not playing or practicing, there was little time to rest and relax. Yao had to face an endless round of requests for interviews, press conferences, photo opportunities, commercials, and personal appearances.

Somehow Yao managed to handle an onslaught of journalists asking him questions in a language he did not know. Speaking through his interpreter, Colin Pine, Yao provided thoughtful and often witty answers to their questions. When asked why he had not dined at any of the Chinese restaurants in Houston, Yao said, "Because there's really good Chinese food at my house."[13] He also told the press that his five favorite words in the English language were "This is the last question."[14]

Yao was able to show an unfailing sense of humor even when he was asked some really silly questions. After a reporter asked Yao why he was so tall, Yao replied, "Can you tell me why you're so small?"[15]

However, handling the press was secondary to proving that he belonged in the NBA. It would take several weeks, but Yao would make his critics and detractors admit they were wrong about him.

FEELING LIKE A ROOKIE

Yao had the decided disadvantage of entering the NBA without spending much time working out and practicing with his teammates. From August 29 to September 8, Yao played for the Chinese team in the International Basketball Federation (FIBA) 2002 World Basketball Championships in Indianapolis.

Yao played well, but China did poorly. They lost seven of eight games and finished twelfth among the sixteen teams competing. During those eight games Yao averaged 21 points, 9 rebounds, and 2 blocked shots per game. His performance earned him a spot on the all-tournament team.

Three weeks after the FIBA competition ended,

Yao played for China in the Asian Games in South Korea. The Asian Games lasted until mid-October. When Yao finally got to practice with the Rockets, he showed both great strengths and great flaws. His teammate, Maurice Taylor recalled, "In the first practice we could see that he had a lot of skill, but he was lost. Brand-new system, brand-new rules—he was a rookie, plain and simple."[1]

Yao was able to play in only two preseason games. One of them was against the San Antonio Spurs. In that game veteran stars Tim Duncan and David Robinson teamed up to hold Yao to 6 points. After the game Yao spoke about how difficult playing in the NBA was going to be. "When you watch on TV, it seems easy," Yao observed. "When you're out there playing, it's really difficult. The NBA is not something everyone can do. I felt like a rookie."[2]

Even before playing in a regular season NBA game, Yao was drawing an incredible amount of attention. On October 24, 2002, Yao met former U.S. president George H. W. Bush and China's president Jiang Zemin. A chauffeured limousine transported Yao to the George Bush Presidential Library at Texas A&M University. Bush welcomed Yao as "the newest Texan from China," and President Zemin called Yao "a national treasure."[3]

Yao's long-awaited and much-publicized NBA debut was not a memorable one, even though it drew a huge television audience. When Houston played the Indiana Pacers on October 30, 2002, the game was broadcast by China Central Television. An estimated 287 million households in China watched the game. Yao had been in the United States and practicing with the Rockets for only ten days. He had only played in two preseason games.

Yao was not in the starting lineup. Early in the second quarter, he came off the bench. He played about seven minutes without scoring a point or blocking a shot. He committed one turnover.

After sitting out the third quarter, Yao returned with about ten minutes left in the game. His first shot was a fifteen-foot fadeaway jumper that fell short of the hoop. That was the only shot he took.

Yao made another turnover when he was double-teamed. The Rockets lost, 91–82. Yao finished the game with some unimpressive stats. He did not score any points or block any shots. In eleven minutes he had 2 rebounds, 2 turnovers, and 3 fouls.

Playing for eleven minutes and sitting on the bench for thirty-seven does not give a player much opportunity to show what he can do. Yao did not need to be reminded that it was not a good performance,

Yao Ming dribbles the ball against Jeff Foster of the Indiana
Pacers during a game in Houston on December 18, 2002.

but he also knew that success in the NBA would not come easily.

Yao's debut might have reminded him of the Chinese proverb: "The longest journey must begin with a single step." Yao's first regular season game was that first step. Yao called it a beginning. "I learned that I have a lot to learn and I am just a rookie," Yao acknowledged. "I realize that this is only the beginning. There are some things that I regret. It was disappointing. But there has to be a start for everything, and this a start for me."[4]

Yao's next game was a slightly better. In an 83–74 win over the Denver Nuggets, Yao scored 2 points and grabbed 7 rebounds in thirteen minutes.

Houston coach Rudy Tomjanovich continued to use Yao sparingly in the early part of the long season. After seven games Yao was averaging just over 4 points a game while playing about fourteen minutes a game. At that time, Yao had more turnovers (8) than assists and only 2 blocked shots. Yao had scored in double figures just one time, when he had 10 points in an 88–87 loss to Phoenix.

It was beginning to look like Yao's critics and detractors had been right. Maybe Yao was not ready for the NBA. Maybe he never would be. Perhaps his permanent role would be as a sub, using his height for easy rebounds and put-back baskets off offensive rebounds.

Then on November 17 Yao had a breakout game against the Lakers. In a 93–89 win, Yao scored 20 points in only twenty-three minutes. Yao was perfect from both the floor (9-of-9) and the foul line (2-for-2). He also had 6 rebounds.

Yao's achievement was somewhat diminished because Shaq did not play in the game. The Lakers star center was still recuperating from off-season foot surgery. Still, it showed NBA fans that Yao had the potential to become a dominating player.

After the game Lakers coach Phil Jackson downplayed Yao's numbers by reminding everyone that Shaq was not playing. "[O'Neal] would break him [Yao] in two," Jackson said. "It wouldn't be fair for the kid to go against Shaquille, such a dominant force, such a dynamic amount of energy."[5]

Laker players Rick Fox and Kobe Bryant did not talk about what a difference Shaq would have made; they both talked about Yao's outstanding game and his vast potential to become even better.

"He added to his highlight reel tonight," Fox said. "He's been a much maligned No. 1 draft pick. You can't teach 7-6. This is an individual who can clearly

Yao Ming puts a shot up over two defenders during a game against the Atlanta Hawks in December 2002.

play the game; he's no circus act. He's going to have more and more nights like this."[6]

Kobe suggested that the only thing that could limit Yao would be Yao's mental attitude. "He has all the skills to be effective in this league," Bryant said. "It's just a matter of his determination, his confidence, and his belief in himself. He hurt us tonight. We were soft in the middle and he took advantage tonight."[7]

Yao quickly showed Jackson and any remaining critics that his performance against the Lakers was no fluke. Two games after the win over Los Angeles, Yao scored 30 points against the Dallas Mavericks. Although the Rockets lost, 103–90, many fans thought it was the best game of Yao's young career.

BEST GAME

Less than three weeks after making his NBA debut, Yao showed everyone that he could put up some big numbers. He also showed that even though an individual can have outstanding game, his team could still lose. In a breakout game against the Dallas Mavericks, Yao scored 30 points, grabbed 16 rebounds, and blocked 2 shots in just thirty-three minutes of play. Still, the Rockets lost to the Dallas Mavericks, 103–90.

The game was one of those rare times when Yao was guarded by someone as tall as, if not taller than, himself. Dallas center Shawn Bradley is 7-6, and Yao has been variously listed as being either 7-5 or 7-6.

Whatever height advantage Bradley had, it did not help him stop Yao from having an outstanding performance. Trying to stop Yao also kept Bradley from doing much scoring or rebounding himself. Bradley finished the game with no points and only 2 rebounds.

Late in the first quarter Yao impressed the fans with a display of defense and hustle. Yao started a fast break by blocking a shot by Steve Nash. Yao's teammate, Cuttino Mobley, grabbed the loose ball and drove to the hoop. Mobley missed a layup by putting the ball up too hard against the backboard. A Dallas player tipped the loose ball. Yao had been trailing Mobley, and he got the tipped ball. Yao quickly stopped, jumped, and swept the ball into the hoop. In less than eight seconds Yao recorded a blocked shot and a basket.

Twenty-one seconds later, Yao was fouled while getting a defensive rebound. He made both shots. In less than thirty seconds, he had a blocked shot, a rebound, and had scored 4 points. One minute later, Yao scored again on an alley-oop pass from Eddie Griffin. Yao finished the first quarter with 9 points.

In the second quarter the Mavericks tried to contain Yao by fouling him. That did not work. Yao went 7-for-7 in foul shooting in the first half. Later in the

Yao Ming tries to get his shot past the outstretched arm of Shawn Bradley of the Dallas Mavericks on November 21, 2002, in Dallas.

second quarter Yao dazzled the crowd with a left handed lay-in while Bradley futilely tried to keep Yao away from the basket.

Jeff Van Gundy, who would later become Yao's coach, was then working as a television analyst. After watching Yao move Bradley out of the way, Van Gundy exclaimed, "That's post-up basketball! [Yao] takes somebody right through the hoop. He just drove Bradley right under the hoop . . . I can see why everyone wanted this guy! . . . This is some show that he's putting on."[1]

After showing some finesse, Yao showed some aggressiveness. He scored on a rim-jarring dunk over Bradley. The dunk was Yao's 29th basket in his last 33 shots. Television commentator Marv Albert noted Yao's shooting streak by remarking, "I would think that you have to go back to the days of Wilt Chamberlain, when a player has put together that kind of run."[2] In 1967 Chamberlain set an NBA record by making 35 consecutive shots.

Unfortunately, Yao's teammates were not shooting very well that night. Mobley, Griffin, Maurice Taylor, and Jauquin Hawkins combined to go 6-for-32 with their shooting. After the game Yao made it clear that winning was still more important to him than his individual performance. "You have to understand,

Yao Ming and Shawn Bradley jockey for floor position.

I play the game in two parts," Yao explained. "One part is the enjoyment of playing. The other part is, of course, winning. Today I achieved half of that."[3]

Yao was 10-of-12 from both the field and the foul line. He complemented his scoring with 16 rebounds and 4 blocked shots in thirty-three minutes. There was one other thing Yao achieved in that game. He would no longer be coming into the game from off the bench. After his outstanding perform-ance, Yao became the Rockets starting center.

> "You have to go back to . . . Wilt Chamberlain, when a player has . . . that kind of run."
> —Marv Albert

Even with Yao starting, Houston was not able to win games consistently. After going on a winning streak, the Rockets would follow it with a losing streak. In mid-December the Rockets enjoyed a three-game winning streak with wins over Miami, Indiana, and Atlanta. That was immediately followed by a three-game los-ing streak to Minnesota, Utah, and New York.

A month later, the Rockets went on a four-game winning streak that improved their record to 23–15. If they could finish out the year by winning half of their remaining games (22-of-44), Houston would have a 45–37 record. That would have all but ensured the Rockets a trip to the playoffs.

Instead of building on the streak, however, the Rockets followed the wins with four consecutive losses. In two of those losses, Yao scored only 10 points. Following that loss streak, the Rockets went 7–11. That dropped their record to 30–30.

Whether the Rockets were winning or losing, one thing did not change—the demands on Yao's off-court time and the worldwide interest in Yao. While adjusting to a new league, a new country, and a new culture, Yao appeared in commercials for Apple Computers, Gatorade, and Visa. Yao also appeared on the cover of numerous magazines including *Time*, *Sports Illustrated*, *Slam*, and *ESPN*.

Because of his extreme height, Yao became an instantly recognizable celebrity. Lisa Ling, the host of the *National Geographic Ultimate Explorer* television show, compared Yao's life to pop star Britney Spears's.

"He's probably one of the most swamped people in the world," Ling said. "The press follows him everywhere. I've been out with Britney Spears and other huge celebrities, but no one has gotten the kind of attention that Yao has. It's incredible. He can't exactly put on a hat and glasses and blend into the crowd."[4]

There were also special promotions by other NBA teams when the Rockets were on the road. When the

Yao Ming tries to get a hand on the ball as Shawn Bradley drives to the basket.

Rockets traveled to Miami, the Heat promoted Yao's appearance by giving away free fortune cookies to everyone attending the game. It was considered an unusual promotion because fortune cookies are more common in America than they are in China. They were invented by Chinese immigrants in San Francisco in the early 1900s. Fortune cookies weren't introduced into China until the 1990s, and they were usually served to foreign tourists instead of native Chinese.

When asked about the unique promotion, Yao said, "First of all, there's no such thing as a fortune cookie in China. Second, I think that fortune cookies are too small. They should give out something bigger."[5]

ALL-STAR

The voting for the 2003 All-Star Game was yet another indication of how much worldwide attention Yao was drawing during his rookie NBA season. Fans logging on to the NBA official Web site to vote for the starting lineups were able to vote in Chinese, Spanish, and seven other languages.

This new, inclusive policy was criticized by those who thought the balloting had become too much of a popularity contest. Since China had a population of around 1.3 billion people, there were concerns that Yao would be chosen as the starting center for the Western Conference and Shaq would become a reserve player.

Yao acknowledged that a lot of his countrymen would vote for him, and he was honored by their votes. Still, he graciously said that Shaq should be the starter. "[Shaq's] the best center in the game," Yao said. "Why can't he start and I come off the bench?"[1]

Shaq did not act very concerned about the voting. Since he had been the MVP on three consecutive NBA championship teams, it did not seem quite right that a largely untested rookie would be starting. Shaq merely said that Yao was making history for his people and that it was hard to beat someone from a country that large. "His people are proud of him [Yao]," Shaq said. "They should be. One billion people—that's tough to beat."[2]

Yao didn't get anything close to a billion votes, but he did beat out Shaq by a large margin. The final vote was Yao 814,393, Shaq 655,744. Yao became the sixteenth rookie and the first international player to start in the All-Star Game.

Shaq downplayed the voting and said that starting was not that important to him. "It really doesn't matter whether I start for the All-Star team, because I've done it many times before," Shaq said. "All I'm interested in now is winning championships."[3]

Shaq ended up playing more minutes (twenty-six)

Tracy McGrady splits defenders Yao Ming and Tim Duncan on his way to the basket during the NBA All-Star Game played in Atlanta, Georgia, on February 9, 2003.

than Yao (seventeen) and having a bigger overall impact on the game. Shaq finished with 19 points, 13 rebounds, 2 steals, and a blocked shot. Yao only took one shot and scored 2 points while getting 2 rebounds with no steals, assists, or blocked shots.

Both of their performances were overshadowed by Kevin Garnett's MVP outing. Garnett led the West to a 155–145 double overtime win by scoring 37 points, with 9 rebounds, 3 assists, 5 steals, and a blocked shot.

Yao was happy just to be there, but he expected to play more in future All-Star matchups. "It was a lot of fun tonight. It was like attending a party. I didn't mind the lack of playing time. It's just something that makes everybody happy and gives people something to watch. . . . Of course I wouldn't mind playing more. But I think in the future, I'll have more of an opportunity."[4]

TIME-OUT

On April 16 the Rockets played their final regular season game. They finished with a 43–39 record. That was a vast improvement over the 2001–02 season when they were 28–54. Still, it was not good enough to get them into the playoffs. The Phoenix Suns, led by rookie sensation Amare Stoudemire, grabbed the eighth and last Western Conference spot in the NBA Playoffs.

Stoudemire also bested Yao in the voting for NBA Rookie of the Year honors, but Yao was named the league's rookie of the year by the *Sporting News*, *Sports Illustrated*, and *ESPN*. He was also a unanimous selection for the NBA's All-Rookie team.

Yao Ming attempts to block the shot of Amare Stoudamire of the Phoenix Suns on January 15, 2003. Stoudamire beat out Yao for Rookie of the Year honors in 2003.

After six months of nonstop travel, interviews, games, practices, and other demands on his time, Yao wanted to enjoy a well-earned rest. After returning to his off-season home in Shanghai, Yao hoped to have about a month off before starting practice with the Chinese men's basketball team in late May. "The holiday will be quite long, and I will try out all the local snacks at this time," Yao said with a smile. "However, the first thing I want to do now is sleep."[1]

Yao's hopes for some rest and relaxation were abruptly ended because an epidemic of severe acute respiratory syndrome (SARS) was sweeping through China. As China's best-known and most respected professional athlete, Yao felt an obligation to do something about the widespread menace to public health. "I just feel there is an obligation as a celebrity to repay society and lead the way for other Chinese basketball players to do more in the way of community service," Yao explained. "This is a great opportunity to do that and a great cause."[2]

The three-hour telethon that Yao hosted included videotaped messages from NBA stars Shaquille O'Neal, Allen Iverson, Tim Duncan, Tracy McGrady, and Steve Nash. Yao autographed hundreds of pairs of shoes to be auctioned at the telethon. There were also signed sports memorabilia from Michael Jordan,

New York's Patrick Ewing puts up a shot during the 1994 NBA Finals against Houston. The 1994 Finals games were the first NBA games Yao saw on television and he became an instant fan. Ewing would later become one of Yao's coaches.

Tiger Woods, and other sports stars. The telethon raised over three hundred thousand dollars for SARS treatment and research.

In late May, Yao learned that his coach, Rudy Tomjanovich, was resigning after being the Rockets head coach for twelve seasons. In March, Tomjanovich had taken a leave of absence from coaching after learning that he had bladder cancer. With Tomjanovich as their head coach, the Rockets had won NBA Championships in 1994 and 1995. After hearing the news, Yao issued a statement from his off-season home in Shanghai: "Rudy has accomplished a great deal during his years with the Rockets, and I feel fortunate to have had the time during my rookie season.[3] Yao added that he considered his former coach to be a "mentor, a role model, and a friend."[4]

About the same time that Tomjanovich was resigning, Yao became involved in a legal dispute with the Coca-Cola Company. Yao had signed a multi-year contract with Pepsi to endorse Gatorade, Pepsi-Cola, and other products made and owned by Pepsi. Coca-Cola had used a photo of Yao and two of his teammates on the Chinese National Team on Coke bottles in China. To show he was not motivated by money, Yao sued for one yuan (about twelve cents) and asked for a public apology.

Coca-Cola's position was that they had a legal right to use Yao's image because they signed a three-year deal with the Chinese Sports Management Company. That company was the agent for the Chinese National Team, and Coca-Cola was one of the team's sponsors. The dispute was settled in late October, when Coca-Cola formally apologized to Yao.

In early June the Rockets announced that former New York Knicks coach Jeff Van Gundy had been hired to succeed Tomjanovich as their head coach. Van Gundy soon hired former Knicks star center Patrick Ewing as an assistant coach. The 7-foot Ewing had been a dominating center and a perennial all-star during his playing days. He was expected to give Yao one-on-one instruction on improving his game.

While practicing with the Chinese National Team, Yao experienced something he had been able to avoid during his NBA rookie season: a significant injury. The injury was variously reported as a cut eyebrow and as a broken bone over his left eye. The injury occurred in late July and kept Yao out of action for about a week.

Yao ended his hectic off-season by leading the Chinese National Team to a 106–96 win over South

Yao Ming takes instructions from Rockets' assistant coach Patrick Ewing during a playoff game on April 28, 2004.

Korea in the championship game of the Asian Men's Basketball championship. Yao was dominating both offensively and defensively. He scored 30 points and grabbed 15 rebounds. Yao's presence in the paint shut off the South Koreans' inside game. They ended up taking 40 shots from behind the three-point line. The win secured the Chinese men's team a berth in the 2004 Summer Olympics in Athens, Greece.

After taking a brief break from basketball, Yao returned to Houston for the 2003–04 NBA season.

SOPHOMORE SEASON

As Yao began his second season he faced some big changes—a new coach, a new uniform, and a glittering new home arena in Houston. But the biggest and best change for Yao came with the rookie debuts of Denver's Carmelo Anthony and Cleveland's LeBron James. The media shifted their attention to the two teenage rookies and away from Yao.

During Yao's rookie season the Rockets had Yao hold a press conference in every NBA city. Now they just made him available to the media when the rest of the team had to do interviews. Still, Yao remained very cautious and at times tight-lipped in dealing with the media.

Yao Ming dunks the ball during a national television game against the Lakers on Christmas day, 2003.

"It has been very interesting this season after having experienced the media crush last year," Yao said in an e-mail to *The Denver Post*. "This year has been much easier. But I still feel that I have to be careful about what I do and say. Yes, the [Anthony-James] rivalry has definitely taken much of the pressure and attention from me. Earlier this year I was asked what I was thankful for this year, and my answer was 'LeBron James.'"[1]

During Yao's rookie season the intrusive media demands, along with the language and cultural differences, set him apart from his teammates. During his second season he enjoyed a greater feeling of acceptance and inclusion. "He's one of the guys," said Rockets teammate Kelvin Cato. "He was one of guys when he got here, but everybody was kind of tiptoeing with him. Now we pal around with him."[2]

The addition of Patrick Ewing to the Rockets' coaching staff gave Yao a coach to work with him one-on-one and teach him how to become a better center and all-around player. During his seventeen-season career in the NBA, Ewing scored over 24,000 points, grabbed over 11,000 rebounds, and blocked over 2,800 shots. In 1996 Ewing was named one of the fifty players on the NBA's exclusive 50th Anniversary All-Time Team.

Yao Ming dribbles past a defender in a game against the Denver Nuggets in Denver, Colorado, on December 26, 2003.

Ewing recognized that Yao is a tremendously talented player and believed that with the right coaching, Yao would get even better:

Right now, Yao is a good player, but he has the size, shooting ability, passing ability, and athletic skills to be up there with Shaq. The main thing he needs is to get closer to the basket. When I played, you could just bull your way in, and the defense would bull you back. The rules have changed, so it takes finesse along with power. . . . Defensively, Yao has to play bigger. He has to use his size to clog up the lane better than he did last year. Put your hands up, hold your position, stay balanced.[3]

Midway through his second season, Yao showed improvement in several areas. His scoring (15.7), rebounding (9.2), and blocks per game (1.9) averages were all up. On the downside, Yao was also averaging more turnovers and fouls per game. The increase in turnovers and fouls has been attributed to Yao being double-teamed more frequently than last season. The biggest criticism of Yao has been that he needs to be more aggressive, especially when he is being double-teamed.

"He needs to elbow somebody in the face when they come down to double-team him the first time," said Coach Van Gundy. "That would be a good start.

Tim Duncan of the San Antonio Spurs tries to block Yao's shot during a game in San Antonio, Texas, on February 24, 2004.

Get them off of him. He's very kind when people come down there."[4]

Coach Ewing worked with Yao on playing against the double-team strategy. "I just basically tried to show him some things to make him more comfortable with the double-team," Ewing said. "Because if he doesn't get better at it, teams are going to do it the whole year. Just basically telling him to either split the double team or try to get the ball to the open man a little earlier and more accurately. But basically, just to use his 7-6 frame to his advantage."[5]

Yao was still inconsistent at times. He followed a mediocre 6-point game against the Celtics with three consecutive games of scoring over 20 points and getting over 10 rebounds. In November he scored 22 points and had 20 rebounds against the Pistons. A month later, Yao had a career-high 7 blocked shots against the Miami Heat.

Barring injury, Yao should enjoy a lengthy and productive NBA career. Whether he will become a dominant center like Bill Russell, Wilt Chamberlain, Kareem Abdul-Jabbar, or Shaq remains to be seen. Until he leads the Rockets to an NBA championship, Yao will likely be regarded as a very good, very tall player whose team was not able to win it all.

10

GROWING INTO HIS GAME

Despite a late season collapse in which they lost seven of their last ten games, the Rockets were able to make the playoffs for the first time in five years in 2004. Yao had been the only member of the Rockets to play in all eighty-two regular season games. He admitted to being fatigued. "I think it [fatigue] has affected me," Yao said. "There are a lot of things that I want to do, but I can't get it done. I worry that if I play like this, it will affect the playoffs."[1]

Houston's 45–37 record made them the seventh-seeded team in the Western Conference Playoffs. They would have to play the Lakers in a first round in a best-of-seven series. The stage was set for another Yao versus Shaq matchup.

The Rockets and Lakers had last faced each other on February 11. Houston had won easily, 102–87. Yao had outscored (29–24) and outrebounded (11–9) Shaq. Still, Shaq proudly insisted that he was the better player. "He made the shots, but he got the whistle too," O'Neal said after fouling out of the game. "I don't think he'll be able to play me one-on-one, ever, ever, ever."[2]

When they met for Game 1, Shaq played like he had something to prove. His 20-point, 10-rebound performance sparked the Lakers to a 72–71 win. Shaq also scored the game-winning basket by moving Yao out of his way and dunking over him. Yao fouled Shaq on the play. That fouled Yao out of the game with seventeen seconds left.

The Rockets got the final shot. Jim Jackson tried a three-point attempt from the left corner, but it clanged off the rim. Shaq grabbed the rebound, and the Lakers went up in the series, 1–0.

In Game 2 Yao made a strong comeback. He scored 21 points while holding Shaq to 7. However, Kobe Bryant (36 points) and Karl Malone (17 points) took up the scoring slack for Los Angeles.

Houston led at the half, 46–44, but the Lakers

Yao Ming muscles his way past the Los Angeles Lakers' Karl Malone during Game 5 of the 2004 NBA Western Conference Quarterfinals on April 28, 2004.

surged in the second half and won, 98–84. Yao acknowledged that the Rockets had a big letdown in the final twenty-four minutes. "In the second half you could tell that our attention slipped and we weren't focused on the game like we were last time," Yao said.[3]

In Game 3 the Rockets enjoyed their first playoff win in five years. Yao keyed the victory by making a crucial left-handed hook shot late in the game. Yao's shot gave Houston a 92–86 lead with 1:51 left. The Rockets went on to win, 102–91.

"It was a great shot against a very good defense," said Rockets coach Jeff Van Gundy. "We needed for that shot to go in."[4]

Whatever lift the Rockets got from that win did not carry over into the rest of the series. In Game 4 Yao fouled out with 1:27 left in overtime. The Lakers went on to win, 92–88. Yao was called for his sixth foul when he was guarding Malone driving to the hoop. Yao, who seldom shows displeasure with a call, asked the officials for an explanation of the call. He did not get one. Afterward, he criticized the crucial call."If that's a foul, then I can't play defense," Yao said.[5]

The Lakers ended the series on their home court with a 97–78 win. Yao held Shaq to 12 points, but

Yao Ming tries to block the shot of Kobe Bryant of the Los Angeles Lakers.

Kobe Bryant's 31 points and 10 assists kept the game from ever being close. In the third quarter the Lakers went on a 33–7 run, and the Rockets never got back into the game. "We were originally floating and we slowly started sinking," Yao said.[6]

After the Rockets were eliminated, Yao acknowledged his shortcomings and the team's lack of confidence. "Overall, we didn't have the resolve," Yao said. "It was a confidence problem. Being young is part of the problem, but we don't want to continue to hide behind that. I just need to learn more."[7]

CHAPTER NOTES

Chapter I. A Giant Matchup

1. Douglas Choi, *The Tao of Yao: Wit and Wisdom from the "Moving Great Wall" Yao Ming* (Seattle: Almond Tree Books, 2003), p. 124.

2. Jack McCallum, "Really Big Show," *Sports Illustrated*, January 27, 2003, p. 62.

3. Ibid.

4. "What Yao Is Saying," *YaoMingMania.com*, n.d., <http://www.yaomingmania.com/#yaosaying> (May 20, 2004).

5. Marty Burns, "Giant Steps," *CNNSI.com*, January 17, 2003, <http://sportsillustrated.cnn.com/inside_game/marty_burns/news/2003/01/17/burns_insider/> (February 10, 2004).

6. Ibid.

7. Michael Murphy, "Yao-Shaq Duel Meets Huge Expectations," *Houston Chronicle*, January 18, 2003, p. 1C.

8. "About His Performance Against Shaq and the Lakers," *YaoMingMania.com*, January 17, 2003, <http://www.yaomingmania.com/quotesfromyao.html> (May 20, 2004).

9. Burns, "Giant Steps."

Chapter 2. Growing Up

1. Jane Yin, "Meet Yao," n.d., <http://www.yaoming.net/meetyao.aspx> (May 20, 2004).

2. Lang Whitaker, "The World Is Yours," *Slam*, May 2003, p. 100.

3. "Big Shot," *Sports Illustrated for Kids*, April 18, 2003, <http://www.yaomingnet/newsfulltext.aspx?nid=97> (May 20, 2004).

4. Henry Abbott, "Yao's Rocket Ride," *Inside Stuff*, May 2003, p. 48.

5. Ibid.

6. Ibid.

7. Ibid.

8. Oliver Chin, *The Tao of Yao: Insights from Basketball's Brightest Big Man* (Berkeley: Frog, Ltd., 2004), p. 3.

9. Ibid.

10. Douglas Choi, *The Tao of Yao: Wit and Wisdom from the "Moving Great Wall" Yao Ming* (Seattle: Almond Tree Books, 2003), p. 19.

11. Ibid.

12. "Beating China Not A Tall Order," n.d., <http://www.usabasketball.com/men/archive/00_moly_recap_china.html> (February 10, 2004).

13. Chin, p. 8.

Chapter 3. Swimming With the Sharks

1. Craig S. Smith, "China Bars Basketball Star from U.S. Event," *The New York Times*, March 30, 2000, p. A6.

2. Ibid.

3. Ibid.

4. Craig S. Smith and Mike Wise, "Eyeing N.B.A., China Will Make Athletes Pay," *The New York Times*, April 25, 2002, p. D4.

Chapter 4. Number One Pick

1. Joe Lago, "Rockets Make Yao First Overall Pick," *ESPN.com*, n.d., <http://sports.espn.go.com/

nbadraft/story?id=1399417> (February 10, 2004).

2. "Yao Ming Profile," *NBADraft.net*, n.d., <http://nbadraft.net/profiles/yaoming.htm> (May 20, 2004).

3. Ibid.

4. Ibid.

5. "'Expert' Hall of Shame," *YaoMingMania.com*, n.d., <http://www.yaomania.com/shame.html> (May 20, 2004).

6. Ibid.

7. Ibid.

8. "Yao Ming Profile," *NBADraft.net*.

9. Don Casey, "Yao Ming Scouting Report," *NBA.com: Draft 2002*, n.d., <http://www.nba.com/draft2002/casey_on_yao.html> (May 20, 2004).

10. "Yao Ming Draft Bio," *ESPN.com*, n.d., <http://sports.espn.go.com/nbadraft/tracker/player?playerId=18333> (May 20, 2004).

11. Oliver Chin, *The Tao of Yao Insights from Basketball's Brightest Big Man* (Berkeley: Frog, Ltd., 2004), p. 71.

12. Marc Stein, "In the End, Can Yao Stand Above the Rest?" *ESPN.com*, January 29, 2002, <http://www.espn.go.com/nba/columns/stein_marc/1500598.html> (May 20, 2004).

13. Douglas Choi, *The Tao of Yao: Wit and Wisdom from the "Moving Great Wall" Yao Ming* (Seattle: Almond Tree Books, 2003), p. 140.

14. Ibid., p. 141.

15. Ibid., p. 147.

Chapter 5. Feeling Like a Rookie

1. John Tyrangiel and Perry Bacon, "The Center of Attention," *Time*, February 10, 2003, p. 68.

2. *Houston Chronicle*, October 24, 2002.

3. Oliver Chin, *The Tao of Yao: Insights from Basketball's Brightest Big Man* (Berkeley: Frog, Ltd., 2004), p. 108.

4. Douglas Choi, *The Tao of Yao: Wit and Wisdom from the "Moving Great Wall" Yao Ming* (Seattle: Almond Tree Books, 2003), p. 67.

5. Mark Heisler, "Pro Basketball; How Now Yao?" *Los Angeles Times*, November 17, 2002, p. D1.

6. "Articles," *YaoMingMania.com*, n.d., <http://www.yaomania.com/articles.html> (February 10, 2004).

7. Ibid.

Chapter 6. Best Game

1. "Articles," *YaoMingMania.com*, n.d., <http://www.yaomania.com/articles.html> (February 10, 2004).

2. Ibid.

3. Douglas Choi, *The Tao of Yao: Wit and Wisdom from the "Moving Great Wall" Yao Ming* (Seattle: Almond Tree Books, 2003), p. 167.

4. Brian Handwerk, "Yao Ming: NBA Giant Is Big in U.S., Bigger in China," *National Geographic News*, May 30, 2003, <http://news.nationalgeographic.com/news/2003/05/0530_030530_yaoming.html> (February 10, 2004).

5. Israel Gutierrez, "Heat Overcomes 14-Point Deficit Before Falling to Rockets in Overtime," *Miami Herald*, December 17, 2002, p. 1D.

Chapter 7. All-Star

1. Sean Deveney, "Bigger and Better," *Sporting News*, January 20, 2003, p. 10.

2. Jonathan Feigen, "Yao Laps Shaq in All-Star Race," *Houston Chronicle*, January 3, 2003, p. 1C.

3. Art Garcia, "NBA Insider: Former A&M Coach Barone Finds Comfortable Seat on Grizzlie's Bench," *Dallas-Fort Worth Star Telegram*, February 16, 2003, p. D8.

4. Janny Hu, "Yao Has Fun Time on All-Star Stage," *Houston Chronicle,* February 10, 2003, p. 1C.

Chapter 8. Time-Out

1. "Yao returns home to Shanghai," n.d., <http://english.eastday.com/epublish/gb/paper1/1887/class000100002/hwz131518.htm> (February 10, 2004).

2. Jonathan Feigen, "Yao to Host Telethon for SARS Treatment," n.d., <http://www.chron.com/cs/CDA/printstory/hts/sports/bk/bkn/rox/1899336> (February 10, 2004).

3. Associated Press, "Yao Ming 'Sorry to Hear' About Tomjanovich's Departure From Coaching," n.d., <http://www.miamiherald.com/mld/miamihearld/sports/5960682.htm> (February 10, 2004).

4. Ibid.

Chapter 9. Sophomore Season

1. Marc J. Spears, "Yao Doesn't Regret Becoming Old News," *Denver Post*, December 26, 2003.

2. Jonathan Feigen, "As Second Season Nears, Yao Is Just One of the Guys," *Houston Chronicle*, October 21, 2003, p. 1C.

3. Jack McCallum, "How to . . . Teach a 7-6 Center If You're a Mere 7-foot Coach," *Sports Illustrated*, October 27, 2003, p. 85.

4. Megan Manfull, "Yao Urged to Send Message," *Houston Chronicle*, January 3, 2004, p. 3C.

5. Ibid.

Chapter 10. Growing Into His Game

1. Jonathan Feigen, "Yao Accepts Playoff Responsibilities," *Houston Chronicle*, April 14, 2004, p. 1C.

2. Associated Press, "Yao Steals Show from Shaq," *Newark Star Ledger* (NJ), February 12, 2004., p.71.

3. "Kobe Carries Lakers in Rout," www.nba.com/games/20040423/LALHOU/recap.html.

4. Ibid.

5. Megan Manfull, "OT Loss Leaves Yao Fit to Be Tied," *Houston Chronicle*, April 26, 2004, p. 12C.

6. "Rockets Lift Off in Game 3," *NBA.com*, April 23, 2004, <http://sportsillustrated.com/2004/basket ball/nba/speiclas/playoffs/2004/04/29/rockets> (May 20, 2004).

7. Ira Winderman, "Rockets Not Centered on Yao," *Fort Lauderdale (FL) Sun-Sentinel*, May 2, 2004, p. 10C.

CAREER STATISTICS

CHINA BASKETBALL LEAGUE

Season	Team	GP	FG%	REB	AST	PTS	PPG
1997–1998	Shanghai	21	.615	175	13	210	10.0
1998–1999	Shanghai	12	.585	155	7	251	20.9
1999–2000	Shanghai	33	.585	480	57	699	21.2
2000–2001	Shanghai	22	.678	426	48	596	27.1
2001–2002	Shanghai	34	.721	645	98	1,102	32.4
TOTALS		122	.651	1,881	223	2,858	23.4

ASIAN CHAMPIONSHIPS

Season	Team	GP	FG%	REB	AST	PTS	PPG
2001	China	8	.724	81	5	101	13.4

GP—Games Played **REB**—Rebounds **PPG**—Points Per Game
FG%—Field Goal **AST**—Assists
Percentage **PTS**—Points

OLYMPIC GAMES

Year	Team	GP	FG%	REB	AST	PTS	PPG
2000	China	6	.639	36	10	63	10.5

NBA

Season	Team	GP	FG%	REB	AST	STL	BLK	PTS	AVG
2002–2003	Houston	82	.498	675	137	31	147	1,104	13.5
2003–2004	Houston	82	.522	735	122	22	156	1,431	17.5
TOTALS		164	.511	1,410	259	53	303	2,535	15.5

GP—Games Played
FG%—Field Goal
　　　Percentage
REB—Rebounds

AST—Assists
STL—Steals
BLK—Blocks
PTS—Points

PPG—Points Per Game
AVG—Average

WHERE
TO WRITE

Mr. Yao Ming
c/o Houston Rockets
The Summit
IO Greenway Plaza
Houston, TX 77046

ON THE INTERNET AT:

http://www.nba.com/playerfile/yao_ming.html

http://www.yaomingfanclub.com

INDEX